Pioneering Ecologists

Debra J. Housel, M.S.Ed.

Life Science Readers: Pioneering Ecologists

Publishing Credits

Editorial Director
Dona Herweck Rice

Associate Editor
Joshua BishopRoby

Editor-in-Chief
Sharon Coan, M.S.Ed.

Creative Director
Lee Aucoin

Illustration Manager
Timothy J. Bradley

Publisher
Rachelle Cracchiolo, M.S.Ed.

Science Contributor
Sally Ride Science™

Science Consultants
Thomas R. Ciccone, B.S., M.A.Ed.,
Chino Hills High School
Dr. Ronald Edwards,
DePaul University

Teacher Created Materials Publishing
5301 Oceanus Drive
Huntington Beach, CA 92649
http://www.tcmpub.com

ISBN 978-0-7439-0592-3

Reprinted 2012

Table of Contents

Who Are Ecologists?

If an ecologist stood in your backyard and saw a crow, she'd find out what it eats. She'd want to know how the food supply limits the number of crows. She'd look for animals that compete with the crow for food and nesting materials. She'd learn how important crows are to the area's foxes and hawks. And she'd predict what would occur if all the crows died.

A **habitat** is where a plant or animal lives. The ways in which the things in a habitat interact form an **ecosystem**. **Ecologists** study ecosystems. They want to know how things fit together in the natural world.

Early ecologists were known as naturalists, or those who studied nature. Much of their work was done through observation. Observing nature remains an important part of ecology today.

Ecologists look at the connections living things have with one another and their surroundings. **Ecology** began as a science in 1866. That's when Ernst Haeckel coined the term. He saw nature as groups of "households." So do today's ecologists. Instead of households, they talk about ecosystems.

Ecology's Roots

Over 800 years ago, a German nun named Hildegard of Bingen wrote about the relationship among humans, plants, animals, and their world. She said that people have a duty to take care of the earth. She also said that the plants and animals living in an area rely on one another. Modern ecology has come to similar conclusions.

John Woodward (1665–1728)

Dr. John Woodward did an experiment in 1699. He put a water mint plant into each of four glass jars. He filled one jar with rainwater. He filled another with muddy water from the Thames River. Into a third jar he put drain water. The last jar had drain water with rotting leaves. He weighed each plant at the start. After 77 days, he weighed them again. This told him how much each had grown.

John Woodward

At the Start of the Experiment

The plant in rainwater increased its mass by 60 percent. The plant in the Thames River water grew 90 percent. The drain water plant increased its weight by 125 percent. And the drain water plant with the rotting leaves grew an amazing 310 percent! Woodward thought that this was due to the amount of soil in the water. Now we know that the rotting leaves broke down into nutrients. Then the plant's roots absorbed them.

Woodward used glass jars and water from different sources in his experiment.

Dueling Doctors

In the early 1700s, even well-educated people used duels to settle scientific disputes! Dr. Woodward wrote an essay called "A Natural History of the Earth and Terrestrial Bodies." It included the results of his experiment. Then he disagreed with another doctor about physics. They held a bloodless sword duel, which Woodward lost. He was thrown out of the Royal Society, a group of the best scientists in England. After that, people paid little attention to his findings.

It was not normal for the last water mint to more than triple its weight in such a short time. If that were to occur in nature, the water mint would take over the body of freshwater. It would choke out other plants and wildlife. Woodward knew that something was up. In nature, the mint plants would be competing for the nutrients in the water. Since the plant was by itself, it ate all the nutrients in the glass and grew huge!

This is what happens with **algae bloom**. Algae bloom looks like green scum floating on water. It occurs when **fertilizer** is put on lawns and farms. After rain, the fertilizer runs off into lakes and ponds. Then the algae have too much food and go wild!

Algae blooms cut the depth to which light can reach. Even worse, the algae lower the water's oxygen levels, and that kills off fish. You can prove this by doing the lab in the appendix.

An algae bloom turns the water green in China's Lake Dian.

Deadly Algae Bloom

Red algae live in saltwater. When they bloom, they produce poison. Scientists call them **HABs** (harmful algae blooms). Few areas of U.S. coastal waters are free of HABs.

Zooplankton (very small animals) eat this bad algae. Then larger fish eat them and die. The fish bodies pile up on beaches, often on the coast of Asia.

Flamingos are the only animals that can safely eat red algae. They have a filter in their bills. It strains the algae from the water. Flamingos keep the number of red algae down. This helps the fish.

flamingo

Aldo Leopold (1887-1948)

Aldo Leopold loved trees. He became a forest ranger and spent years in the woods. Then one day, he did something that changed his life.

Leopold lived in a time when there were no **game laws**. If a person wanted to kill an animal, he could. When Leopold was a young man, he shot a wolf. As he watched it die, he felt guilty. The wolf had not threatened him. He had killed it for no reason! It struck him that every living thing was part of an ecosystem. He had just damaged it without cause.

Leopold urged others to stop killing animals for no reason. It took him years to convince others that wildlife should be preserved. He fought to get laws passed. He became the leader in the field of **game** management. He pushed for game preserves and national forests. He wanted these areas set aside. Then nothing would spoil their natural beauty.

The gray wolf has made a comeback. Ranchers used to shoot wolves because they attacked their cattle. The species was near extinction. Laws were passed to make shooting wolves illegal. Without hunting, the wolf population grew back. Now lawmakers are making new laws to allow just enough wolf hunting to keep their numbers balanced.

These stuffed passenger pigeons can be found in a museum.

Lost Birds

The **extinction** of the passenger pigeon is a shocking story. This bird species was once the most numerous on Earth! Yet they were shot for sport until none were left. The last one died at the age of 29 at a zoo in 1914.

Long ago, dodo birds lived on one island in the Indian Ocean. They could not fly. This made them easy to catch and eat. Pigs came and ate their eggs. By 1680, there were no more dodo birds.

Leopold's work helped create two laws. The first was passed in 1969. It is the National Environmental Policy Act. It states that the government must first think about the **environmental effects** of any land use. This means that a mall cannot be built without a study to find out how to not harm the ecosystem.

The second law is the Endangered Species Act of 1973. It protects plants, animals, and their ecosystems from becoming extinct.

The dodo bird is now extinct. Today's laws may have helped it to avoid **extinction**.

DDT

Rachel Carson was also concerned about animals. She wondered how chemicals affected them. She studied **DDT**. It was sprayed to kill bugs. She found that DDT killed much more than bugs. The birds that ate the bugs were dying, too. Carson said that if people didn't stop using DDT, there would be no birds left. Her 1962 book, *Silent Spring*, made U.S. leaders aware that DDT was dangerous. They banned DDT so no one could use it.

When crops were sprayed with DDT, many people ate the poison. It is stored inside the fat in our glands. When the fat was used, it made people sick.

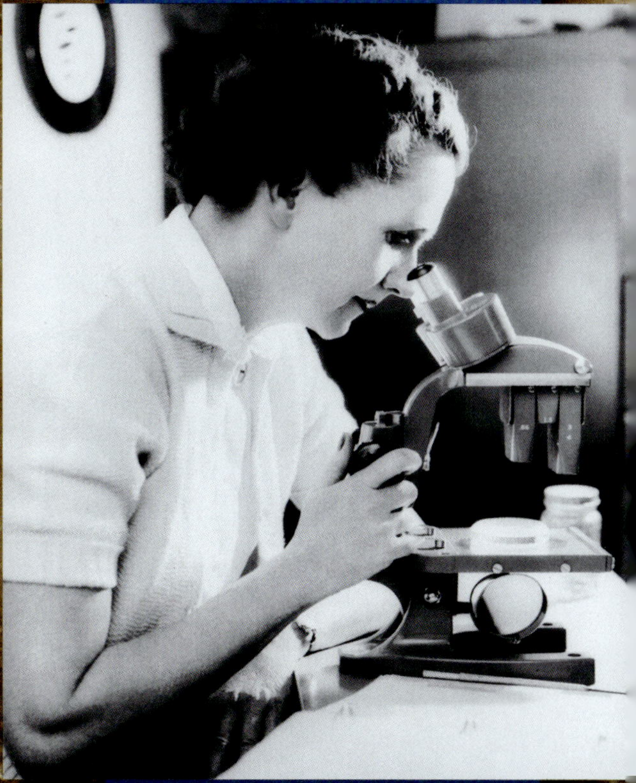

Ruth Patrick (1907–)

Dr. Ruth Patrick

More Salt?

Dr. Patrick proved that Great Salt Lake in Utah was once fresh. It became salty through evaporation.

diatometer

Dr. Ruth Patrick has loved nature since she was young. Her dad took her on walks. They would pick up things. Then they looked at them under a microscope. When she grew up, she started the science of **limnology**. It is the study of freshwater ecosystems.

Patrick was the first to determine the health of a river or stream. She did this by collecting **diatoms** (DAHY-uh-tomz). These are single-celled algae. They are a basic food source for things living in freshwater. Different diatoms prefer different environments. So, their presence is linked to water quality.

To get diatoms, Patrick invented a device. It is called a **diatometer** (DAHY-uh-TOM-ee-ter). It shows the presence of pollution in freshwater. First it is placed in the water. Then it is anchored to the bottom. A cork keeps it afloat. As the water moves through it, diatoms attach to glass slides. The slides are removed and studied.

Ecologists today still use her methods. They measure changes in amounts and kinds of plants, animals, and bacteria. This lets them gauge the impact of pollution. They can also detect other changes.

diatom

Eugene Odum (1913–2002)

In the early 1950s, Eugene Odum worked on a team with Ruth Patrick. The team gathered data about the water quality and things living in the Savannah River. The things he learned there helped him to form important ideas about ecology. Dr. Eugene Odum may be the most important ecologist of the 20th century.

Dr. Eugene Odum

It is easy to find different organisms—plants and animals—interacting.

Odum said that studying one species wasn't taking a broad enough view. He saw Earth as a set of interlocking ecosystems. He urged people to study the ecosystem as a whole. At first, this idea had little support. It is now accepted throughout the world.

Bird Lover

Even as a child, Dr. Odum loved to watch birds. While he was in college, he invented a device to measure a bird's heartbeat. Have you ever spent an afternoon birdwatching?

a wetlands

In 1953, Odum wrote the first ecology textbook. Today, *Fundamentals of Ecology* is still in print. It states that scientists must look at **climate**, plants, and animals to learn how the pieces fit together. His book showed people how to study the ways in which living things are related.

Odum was the first to study salt-marsh plants and animals. He found out how they all use the same nutrients, one after another. They also use the same elements, such as carbon and nitrogen. His research on salt marshes led to laws that protect **wetlands**.

Salt Marsh Nature Center in New York

Why We Need Wetlands

Wetlands include swamps, marshes, and bogs. Swamps have standing water. They are filled with woody plants.

Marshes have grassy plants. Saltwater marshes rely on the tides. When the water rushes out of the marsh, it washes away dead plants and animals. This carries nutrients into the sea.

Bogs have damp soil. Rice grows in bogs. Half of Earth's human population eats rice each day.

Wetlands also hold lots of water. This prevents floods. People have filled in wetlands to build cities. Many animals have lost their homes. Nearly one third of all of America's **endangered** species live in wetlands.

Jane Lubchenco (1947-)

Dr. Jane Lubchenco

Many scientists think that greenhouse gases have raised Earth's surface temperature. They call this **global warming**. They worry that species may become extinct as the climate changes. Dr. Jane Lubchenco brought this problem to the public's attention. She explained it so that people could understand.

Lubchenco has also improved our knowledge of the sea. She has voiced concern for all the world's **coral reefs**. She fears that they all may die within the next 50 years. Her efforts have made the environment an important political issue.

Lubchenco stresses that we must take better care of Earth. She discovered **dead zones** in lakes. Dead zones are places where no fish live. Algae blooms cause dead zones. She has found 40 of them. Each one is near the mouth of a river that has fertilizer runoff.

A dead zone doesn't allow life to prosper in water bodies.

It's Alive!

Coral reefs are alive. When lots of coral polyps grow on top of one another, they build a colorful reef. A huge reef takes half a million years to build. People can hurt the reefs much faster than they can grow.

Dr. Lubchenco taught a class on coral reefs in Jamaica. When she returned more than 10 years later, she found the reefs ruined. Some people dropped bombs into the reef to catch more fish!

Pollution is also a problem. Coral polyps eat algae. Water pollution blocks the sun that the algae need. Global warming kills algae, too. When the algae dies, the coral starves. It dies and turns white. White reefs never recover.

Neo Martinez (1958-

Neo Martinez works in a special lab in Berkeley, California. He uses computers to run simulations. He found the basic things shared by all ecosystems. He came up with a way to explain and picture **food webs**.

This common parasite is a tick.

Most animals eat more than one kind of food. Then those animals are often eaten by more than one kind of **predator**. Imagine you drew all the plants and animals in an area. Then imagine drawing lines from each one to all the organisms it eats. You would have a very complicated web of lines. Martinez calls these networks of lines food webs.

Most animals are predators of some animals and **prey** for others. For example, a wolf is the predator for other animals. But it is the prey of parasites such as **heartworms**. A **parasite** is an animal that lives off a host. The **host** is another animal's body. The parasite may kill its host.

Energy Pyramid

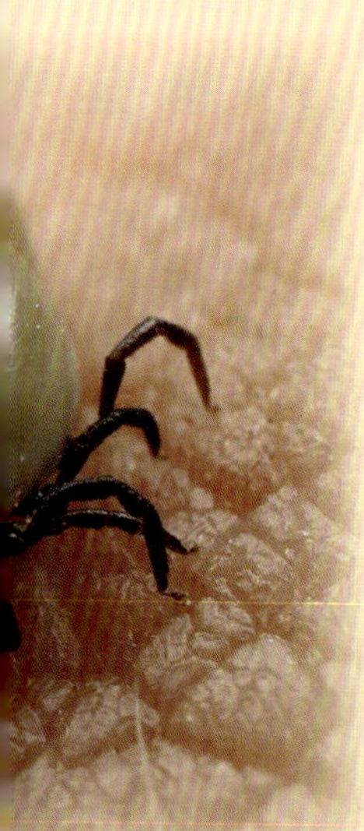

An energy pyramid shows the exchange of energy among organisms in an ecosystem. Organisms get energy from other organisms by eating them. The bottom of the pyramid is made of producers. They are usually plants. The plants provide food for primary consumers such as zebras and gazelles. The primary consumers, in turn, provide food for secondary consumers such as lions.

As the pyramid narrows to the top, the number of consumers decreases. It takes a lot of food to feed the animals on the top. For example, in one year, it takes 7,494 tons (6,798 metric tons) of grass in an area to keep 61 tons (55 metric tons) of primary consumers alive. And that amount of primary consumers keeps just one 450-pound (204 kg) lion alive.

Energy decreases as you move up the pyramid. Every time something gets eaten, energy is lost. There is only enough energy for a few animals at the top.

When looking at an energy pyramid, keep in mind that it doesn't tell the whole story that a food web tells. Many more plants and animals are involved in the exchange of energy in an ecosystem than the plants and animals shown in the pyramid.

One of Martinez's big findings is that many animals are **omnivores**. Omnivores eat both plants and animals. People once thought that most animals were either meat eaters or plant eaters.

Martinez found that small food webs are fragile. The removal or addition of a species can make the whole ecosystem fall apart. For example, the Arctic food web is small. Algae grow on the bottom of the ice. It is eaten by zooplankton. Zooplankton is eaten by small fish. The fish are food for Arctic

Food Web

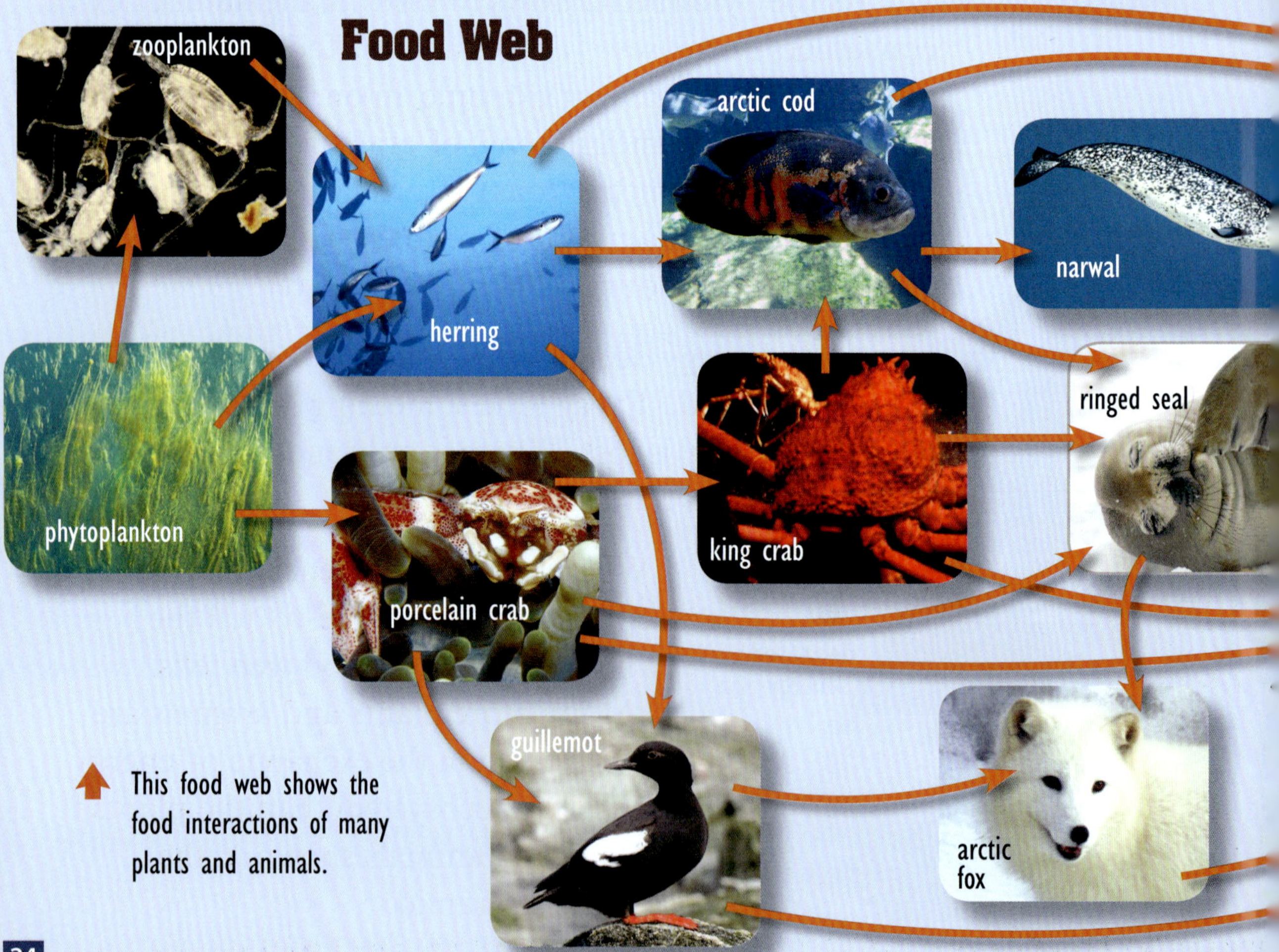

This food web shows the food interactions of many plants and animals.

cod, which are eaten by ringed seals. Polar bears eat the seals.

This food web is in danger from the warming of the Arctic. As ice melts, fewer algae may grow. Then the ecosystem might collapse.

Alien Invaders!

People have caused whole food webs to change. How? By bringing a new species into an ecosystem. These alien species spread quickly. For example, brown tree snakes got onto a ship. The snakes traveled from their home in coastal Australia to the island of Guam. After they arrived, no animals wanted to eat them. Their numbers grew out of control. They wiped out many native birds, small mammals, and lizards.

In Africa, small purple plants choked out animals, too. These water plants filled Lake Victoria. The plants grew into a big blanket. It trapped fishing boats. People couldn't fish. Some scientists use beetles to eat these plants. Others chop the plants with a big machine.

Environmental Mapper: Marie Lynn Miranda

Marie Lynn Miranda and daughter

Life-Saving Maps

Can a map come to the rescue? Sure! Just ask Marie Lynn Miranda. She makes computerized maps that can show hidden dangers.

"As a kid, I *loved* maps," Miranda says. When her family traveled to a new city, she figured out where things were. Later she became interested in protecting children from toxic chemicals. That's when her childhood hobby turned into her career.

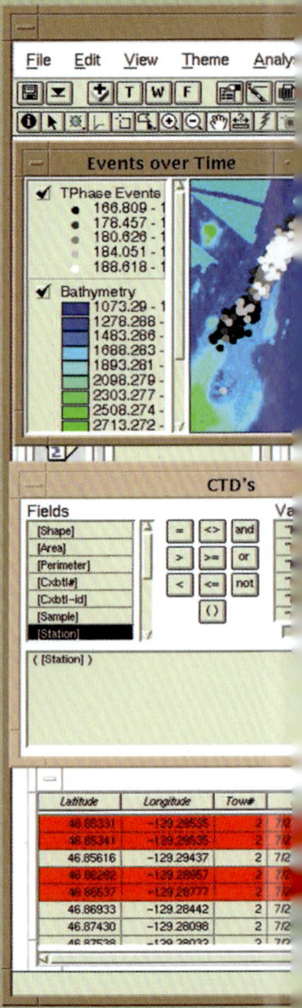

Miranda likes helping kids stay healthy in many ways. "I love coaching young children in soccer and baseball," she says.

For one project, Miranda created a map of a flooded city. First, she added schools to a map of the area. Then she showed places where the floods had spread dangerous chemicals. When she put it all together, presto! The map showed all the schools that were not safe.

Maps, kids, and the environment: it all clicks! "All the pieces of my life fell into place," says Miranda.

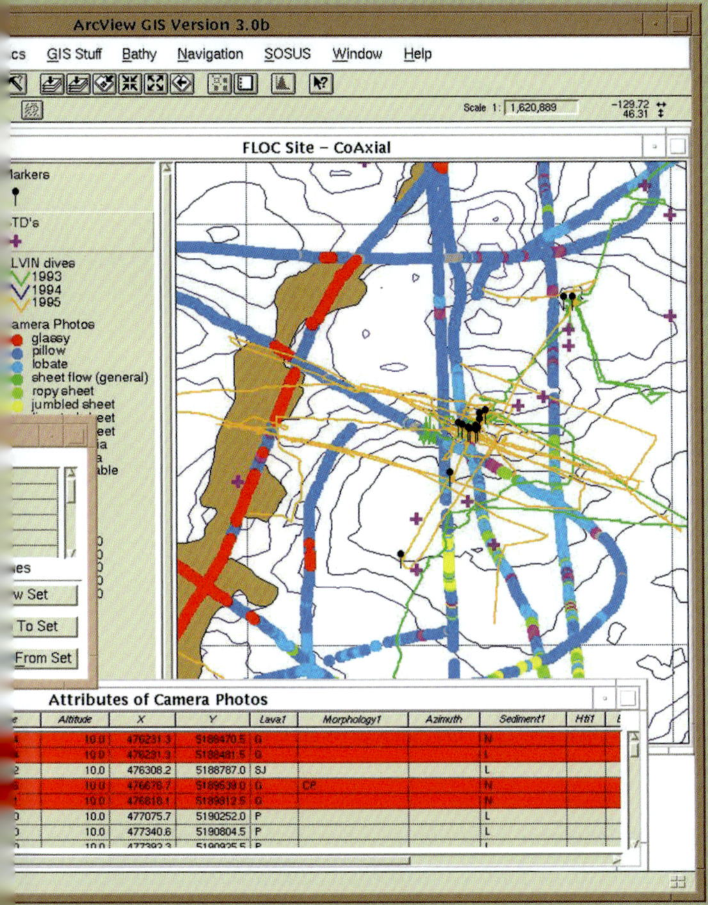

one of Miranda's maps

Think About It

Imagine the perfect map of your neighborhood. What special information would you put on it?

Is It 4 U?

Do you like to draw your ideas on paper? Do you ever wonder about the effect of something, such as pollution?

Being There

Environmental mappers create maps with different types of helpful information. Miranda's maps show places where toxic chemicals may harm children. If you were a mapper, you could help solve questions such as . . .

- Does smoke from a factory harm people living nearby?
- Will a new softball park be too windy in the spring?
- Does logging change the types of animals that live in the forest?

Lab: Creating an Algae

In this experiment, the jar is a freshwater body such as a pond or a lake. The fertilizer is the same as what runs off from treated lawns and farmer's fields when it rains. The sunlight is the same that would shine down on the body of freshwater in nature.

Materials

- freshwater from a pond or a lake (can use tap water, but it will slow down the experiment)
- two clean clear glass jars with a screw-type metal lid (16 oz. jar is ideal)
- liquid lawn or crop fertilizer
- floating water plants (tablespoon of algae from a pond works best)
- $\frac{1}{4}$ teaspoon measure
- masking tape
- pen

Procedure

1 Fill the two glass jars with pond or lake water.*

***** *If you cannot obtain untreated freshwater, you can use tap water. However, because tap water has been treated, it will slow down the experiment.*

2 Place a floating water plant or some algae in each jar.

3 Use the masking tape and pen to label one jar Pond Water and the other jar Fertilized Water.

4 Place $\frac{1}{4}$ teaspoon of liquid lawn fertilizer in the jar labeled Fertilized Water. Stir it thoroughly with the measuring spoon.

5 Place both the jars in sunlight.

6 Observe the jars daily, and record what you see in each.

7 After one week, place another $\frac{1}{4}$ teaspoon of liquid lawn fertilizer in the Fertilized Water jar.

8 Observe the jars and record your observations at the end of the second week.

Conclusion

You will see that the pond plants in the Pond Water jar are growing at a normal pace. The water beneath the plants is relatively clear. The pond plants in the Fertilized Water jar are growing rapidly and taking up all the space. The water below them is cloudy and murky. If there were fish in that jar, they would die due to the plant overgrowth.

Glossary

algae bloom—a green scum of plant matter that covers the surface of freshwater and cuts down on the light oxygen available to aquatic wildlife; caused by high concentrations of nitrate

climate—the typical weather conditions in a particular area

coral reef—an important ecosystem found in warm, shallow parts of the ocean; provides a home for thousands of sea animals

DDT—a spray used to kill harmful insects, also causing the death of many creatures further up the food chain

dead zone—an area in a lake or pond where no fish can live

diatom—single-celled algae that live in freshwater

diatometer—a device for collecting diatoms (single-celled organisms)

ecologist—a scientist who studies ecology

ecology—the relatively new science that looks at the connections that living things have with one another and their surroundings

ecosystem—the interaction between a community of plants and animals living in a natural environment

endangered—a plant or animal that is in such small numbers that it may become extinct

environmental effects—the environmental impact (positive or negative) of development and land use

extinction—the state of a species being completely gone, never to return

fertilizer—any substance put on fields or lawns to make crops or grass grow better, and most often containing nitrate

food web—a series of interlocking food chains that show who eats whom in an ecosystem

game—wild animals, birds, and fish hunted for food and sport

game laws—restrictions on the hunting, trapping, or capture of wild game, whether bird, animal, or fish

global warming—the rising surface temperature of Earth caused by increasing amounts of carbon dioxide and other greenhouse gases in the atmosphere

HAB—acronym for Harmful Algae Bloom, type of saltwater algae that poison the animals that consume them

habitat—the natural home of an animal or a plant

heartworm—a parasite that lives within the heart of its host and eventually results in the host's death

host—the plant or animal from which a parasite gets its nutrition

limnology—the study of freshwater ecosystems

omnivore—an animal that eats both plants and animals

parasite—a plant or animal that gets its food by living on or inside another plant or animal

predator—an animal that hunts and eats other animals (for example, a toad is a bug's predator)

prey—an animal that is eaten by another

wetlands—a large area of land covered with swamp or marsh

zooplankton—tiny animal organism

Index

Sally Ride Science

Sally Ride Science™ is an innovative content company dedicated to fueling young people's interests in science. Our publications and programs provide opportunities for students and teachers to explore the captivating world of science—from astrobiology to zoology. We bring science to life and show young people that science is creative, collaborative, fascinating, and fun.

Image Credits

Cover: Zygimantas Cepaitis/Shutterstock; p.3 Gary Detonnancourt/Shutterstock; p.4 (left) Jan Martin Will/Shutterstock; p.4 (right) Lebrecht Music and Arts Photo Library/Alamys; p.5 Chris Fourie/Shutterstock; p.5 (right) Mary Evans Picture Library/Alamy; p.6 (top) Leonid Nishko/Shutterstock; p.6 (left) Rick Reason; pp.6–7 Lesley Palmer; p.7 (right) Rasmus Rasmussen/iStockphoto; p.8 Bob Sacha/CORBIS; p9 (left) Kristian_Sekulic/Shutterstock; p.9 Chin Kit Sen/Shutterstock; p.10 (top) Photos.com; p.10 (left) CORBIS; p.10 (bottom) Ron Hilton/Shutterstock; p.11 BRUCE COLEMAN INC./Alamy; p.12 The Natural History Museum/Alamy; p.13 (right) Underwood & Underwood/CORBIS; p.13 Photofusion Picture Library/Alamy; p.14 (top) Photos.com; p.14 (left) Raymond Holman; p.14 (bottom) J. W. Sherman/ANSP; p.15 Photos.com; p.16 (top) Neo Edmund/Shutterstock; p.16 (left) John Loengard/Time Life Pictures/Getty Image;s p.16 (bottom) Losevsky Pavel/Shutterstock; p.17 Zygimantas Cepaitis/Shutterstock; p.18 (top) Romeo Koitmäe/Shutterstock; p.18 (bottom) Dmitriy Aseev/Shutterstock; p.19 Anne Kitzman/Shutterstock; p.20 (top) Anne Kitzman/Shutterstock; p.20 (left) Oregon State University; p.20 (bottom) Laurence Lowry/Photo Researchers, Inc.; p.21 Dennis Sabo/Shutterstock; p.21 (top) Yang Xiaofeng/Shutterstock; p.22 (top) sgame/Shutterstock; p.22 (left) Courtesy of Dr. Neo Martinez; pp.22–23 David Dohnal/Shutterstock; p.23 (left) Lesley Palmer; p.24 (zooplankton) Andrew Syred/Photo Researchers, Inc.; p.24 (phytoplankton) Laura Lohrman Moore/Shutterstock; p.24 (herring) Dennis Sabo/Shutterstock; p.24 (porcelain crab) Photos.com; p.24 (arctic cod) William Attard McCarthy/Shutterstock; p.24 (king crab) Rightend/Flickr; p.24 (pigeon guillemot) William Attard McCarthy/Shutterstock; p.24 (narwhal) Richard Ellis/Photo Researchers, Inc.; p.24 (ringed seal) Raldi Somers/Shutterstock; p.24 (arctic fox) Photos.com; p.25 (orca) Anson Hung/Shutterstock; p.25 (polar bear) Nik Niklz/Shutterstock; p.25 Michael & Patricia Fogden/CORBIS; p.26 Duke University; p.27 NOAA; p.28 (top) Anthony Hall/Shutterstock; pp.28–29 Nicolle Rager Fuller, p.32 Getty Images